THE BOOK OF
GODDESSES

THE BOOK OF
GODDESSES

words and pictures by

KRIS WALDHERR

introduction by

LINDA SCHIERSE LEONARD

**BEYOND
WORDS**
Publishing
I N C

Beyond Words Publishing, Inc.,
4443 N.E. Airport Road
Hillsboro, Oregon 97124-6074
503-693-8700/1-800-284-9673

Library of Congress Catalog Card Number: 95-77947

ISBN: 1-885223-30-7

Printed in Singapore by Tien Wah Press (Pte.) Ltd
Distributed to the book trade by Publishers Group West
For a free catalog of other titles by Beyond Words Publishing, Inc., please write
to us at the address above or call our toll-free number, 1-800-284-9673

For Tom

Many people helped and encouraged me while I worked on this book; it is with heartfelt thanks that I acknowledge them.

Barbara Mathé from the Metropolitan Museum of Art's Robert Goldwater Library assisted with research, as did anthropologist Thomas Ross Miller, Melanie Hope Greenberg, and Anne MacFarlane from HarperCollins Australia. Most of the picture research was conducted at the New York Public Library and Brooklyn Public Library in New York City.

My interns, Rebecca Smith and Letecia Stewart, took care of many tasks responsibly and efficiently, enabling me to work on this project uninterrupted. Dianne Clouet, Ellen Dreyer, Nilka Dunne, Stephanie Forest, Wendy Froud, Melanie Hope Greenberg, Cheryl Hanna, Marja Lee, Tom Miller, Patrice Silverstein, and Letecia Stewart modeled for the pictures. Many thanks also to all the enthusiastic people at Beyond Words.

But most of all, I would like to thank Tessa Strickland and Nancy Traversy from Barefoot Books England, where this book originated, for their support, dedication, and belief in this book and its creator.

INTRODUCTION

When I first saw Kris Waldherr's beautifully illustrated book of goddesses from around the world, I was excited by this exquisite gift which shows the divine feminine energies and magical images from so many diverse cultures and traditions. I wish that I had had the opportunity to see this inspiring book when I was young and to share it with my mother. Although my mother was an independent, working woman supporting her family, she was still confined by the limited cultural images of women of her time and expected me to fit a role that was contrary to who I was; she didn't know about the goddesses. If she were alive now, I would be thrilled to show her the beauty, individuality, and unique feminine strength that Kris portrays through her dazzling illustrations and poetic retellings of the goddesses' stories. To see so many inspiring and different images that can stimulate the imagination of both children and adults is a special gift for all of us.

I remember one exciting day in junior high school when I first learned there were goddesses. I ran home to tell my grandmother about this extraordinary discovery. The goddesses gave me new and sparkling images for the different ways a woman might choose to live her life. At that time, the Greek goddess, Athena, whose source of enlightenment was an owl, especially stirred my soul. I associated her with my grandmother who had told me that when she was a farm girl she secretly consulted an owl on certain full-moon nights.

Athena, or Minerva as she was called by the Romans, was the goddess of wisdom and justice, a patroness of artistry, and the inventor of the plow and rake. She also inspired architects to design beautiful temples. What a wonderful feminine model for a girl trying to break free from confining roles so that she could do something significant with her life!

No matter what our age, gender, race, or where we live in the world, we all need the inspiration of the goddess for the spiritual and creative revival of our souls. The goddess culture all over the world, through its many images and stories, and its special respect for animals and nature, emphasizes the very qualities we need to embody in our lives for human and ecological survival.

In *The Book of Goddesses*, Kris Waldherr presents us with twenty-six brilliant watercolor pictures and stories of goddesses from all over the world. Her elegant paintings draw us into the unique and magical world of each goddess and inspire us with appreciation for feminine divinity. Each story and picture offers a different way to view and to value the feminine energies in ourselves.

To see and learn about the powerful Yoruba goddess, Oya, ruler of the Niger river, dressed in a brilliant orange gown and pictured with her spirit animal, the antelope, is to discover a patroness of female leadership who can help us to find the right words for healthy communication.

Kuan Yin, revered as the mother of compassion and mercy in the Buddhist tradition, chose to remain on earth until every human being is free from pain. The story of this Chinese goddess provides us with a symbol for courageous loving kindness.

Benzai-ten, a Japanese goddess of beauty, is shown dressed in the waves of a blue-green lake, playing the biwa, a stringed instrument like the mandolin. With the power of music and art, she can charm the dragon king and is able to help men escape those angry dragons that can devour them. Thus, she is honored as the goddess who favors love and marriage.

Diana, the mother of wild animals, goddess of hunting, of wild natural places, and of the mysterious moon, appears in an oak forest with her bow and arrow and her totem animal, the deer. This Roman goddess, whom the Greeks know as Artemis, portrays athletic strength and grace. She helps young girls learn to be independent, connects us with the cycles of nature, and shows us nature's power of nourishment even in the coldest winter, reminding us of the reverence with which we need to honor and trust nature for the renewal of our souls.

I invite you to open *The Book of Goddesses* and to discover these and other enthralling goddesses with Kris as you enter her inspiring global "magic theater." Experiencing these goddesses will help you to discover the creativity, spirituality and new meaning that makes human life whole and the world a healthier place to live in. With its enchanting artistry, *The Book of Goddesses* is a visual delight and a rare and splendid opening into the domain of the divine feminine.

LINDA SCHIERSE LEONARD, PH.D.

A GUIDE TO THE GODDESSES

ATHENA	*ah-THEE-nah*	Greek goddess of wisdom
BENZAI-TEN	*ben-ZAY-ten*	Japanese goddess of music and beauty
CHANG O	*JAHNG oh*	Chinese moon goddess
DIANA	*die-AN-ah*	Roman goddess of hunting and the moon
ESTSANATLEHI	*est-san-AT-lu-hee*	Navajo creation goddess
FREYJA	*FRAY-ah*	Norse goddess of beauty and love
GWENHWYFAR	*GWEN-eh-far*	Welsh goddess of the islands
HSI WANG MU	*SHEE WANG MUH*	Chinese goddess of immortality
ISIS	*EYE-sis*	Egyptian fertility goddess
JUNO	*JOO-noh*	Roman ruling goddess
KUAN YIN	*KWAN yin*	Chinese goddess of compassion
LAKSHMI	*LAKSH-mee*	Indian goddess of prosperity
MAIA	*MAY-yah*	Greek goddess of the spring

The capital letters indicate where the emphasis should fall in each name.

NYAI LORO KIDUL	*Nahi LOW-row KEH-dul*	Javanese goddess of the South Seas
OYA	*oy-YAH*	African goddess of the Niger River
PELE	*PEH-leh*	Hawaiian fire goddess
(Queen of Heaven) INANNA	*ee-NAN-nah*	Sumerian moon goddess
RHIANNON	*REE-an-non*	Celtic horse goddess
SARASVATI	*sa-RAS-vah-tee*	Indian goddess of knowledge
TARA	*TAH-rah*	Tibetan goddess of mercy
UKEMOCHI	*U-kee-MOH-chee*	Japanese goddess of food
VENUS	*VEE-nus*	Roman goddess of love
WAWALAK	*WAH-wah-lak*	Aboriginal sister goddesses
XOCHIQUETZAL	*sho-chee-KET-sal*	Mexican flower goddess
YEMANA	*yay-MAN-ah*	Cuban Santeria goddess
ZORYA	*ZOR-yah*	Slavic guardian goddesses

ATHENA

Athena (*ah-THEE-nah*), the goddess of wisdom, was one of the most powerful of the ancient Greek goddesses. She was the daughter of Zeus, the Greek father god, and his first wife, Metis, whose name meant "wisdom." Metis warned Zeus that the first son they produced would grow to be more powerful than Zeus himself. Zeus was so agitated by this that when she became pregnant, he swallowed Metis and their unborn child whole. After this huge meal, he had a terrible headache, which was relieved only when he split his head open with an axe. From the wound rushed forth Athena, already fully grown.

Athena came to be revered not only as the goddess of wisdom but also as the goddess of war. Skilled without equal in the art of battle, she gave just protection to those in need of defense, especially to Achilles, the hero of *The Iliad*. Her brilliance of reason was said to be as penetrating as her clear, gray eyes; her artistry in all crafts, especially weaving and pottery, was unrivaled. Once, Athena was challenged to a weaving contest by a woman named Arachne. When Arachne lost, the goddess transformed her into a spider.

Often depicted with an owl as a symbol of enlightenment and a serpent as a symbol of fertility, Athena is credited with the invention of the plow and the rake, which helped humans to cultivate food. She also inspired architects to create elegant temples. Many of these were strong enough to provide security in times of war for the citizens in whose towns they were built.

Athena gave her name to Athens, the capital city of Greece. Then Poseidon, god of the seas, grew jealous of her popularity there and proposed a contest: whoever gave the most valuable gift to the Greeks would become patron of the city. Poseidon gave a saltwater well. But Athena's gift of the olive tree provided shade from the hot sun, oil for lamps, and delicious olives to eat. From that time, all Athenian families have held the olive branch sacred as a symbol of Athena's generosity to them.

BENZAI-TEN

The most beloved deities in Japanese mythology are those that form a group called the Seven Gods of Good Fortune. Of these, the fairy-like Benzai-ten (*ben-ZAY-ten*) is the only goddess. She is believed to bring happiness and wealth to her worshipers. In Japanese art, there are many prints and small statues, especially from the twelfth to the sixteenth century, which show Benzai-ten and her fellow Gods of Good Fortune sailing merrily together on a treasure ship.

Human beings find happiness in many ways. For some people, happiness comes from gaining wisdom and knowledge; others find joy in beauty, music, and art. Benzai-ten is the goddess of all of these wonderful gifts. The middle syllable of her name, *zai*, means "talent" or "wealth" in Japanese. Sometimes she is depicted with eight arms and open hands, symbolizing her many talents and her all-embracing generosity.

Benzai-ten has an interesting pedigree. She is believed to be the daughter of a dragon king. When she grew up, she married another dragon in exchange for his promise to stop eating children. The dragon's love for her cured him of his taste for human flesh. Many people believe that Benzai-ten lives with her dragon husband under the waves of Lake Biwa, which is north of the ancient city of Kyoto. The lake is named after Benzai-ten's favorite instrument, the biwa, a stringed instrument which is like a mandolin. The shape of the lake is similar to that of the biwa.

Many stories tell of Benzai-ten's sympathy for young men who were chased by angry dragons. She is able to help these men escape with their lives because of her close ties with dragons. Other stories praise Benzai-ten's kindness to lovers. Those seeking her help in gaining the favor of a loved one often left beseeching letters on the goddess's shrines. Due to this, Benzai-ten is also considered a goddess of marriage.

CHANG O

Every September, when the full moon is at its most brilliant, the Chinese enjoy a moon festival. This celebration is held in honor of women. It also honors Chang O (*JAHNG oh*), the moon goddess, who is believed to live on the moon with a white rabbit. People bake special, round treats called "moon cakes." As they eat them, they are reminded of the magic potion of immortality that transformed Chang O into the queen of the moon.

Before Chang O became a moon goddess, she lived among the other gods and goddesses with her husband, Yi, the divine archer. But when Yi shot nine suns out of the sky, leaving only one to warm the earth, the unlucky couple were stripped of their immortality and forced to live among humans. Chang O was dismayed. She begged her husband to go and seek the potion of immortality from the goddess Hsi Wang Mu, who made it from her magical peaches. Hsi Wang Mu was sympathetic, so she gave Yi enough for them to become immortal but not enough for them to become god and goddess again.

When Yi returned, Chang O was delighted by his success. But Yi did not want to drink the potion straight away. Instead, he told his wife to watch over it while he went hunting. As time passed, Chang O became more and more agitated. Then she had an idea. If she drank Yi's potion as well as her own, perhaps she would become a goddess again. After all, she reasoned, she was not the one who had shot down the suns, so why should she be punished? Too tempted to resist, she drank the entire potion. Soon, Chang O felt herself becoming lighter and lighter, and she floated away toward the heavens. Before she knew it, she was on the moon, once again a beautiful goddess, but unable to leave because of her weightlessness.

Though Yi was at first angry with Chang O, he did love her and quickly forgave her. To make her more comfortable on the cold moon, he built her a magnificent palace out of fragrant cinnamon wood. But Yi can only visit his wife once a month on the night of the new moon.

DIANA

In ancient Rome, the goddess Diana (*die-AN-ah*) was honored as the mother of the wild animals. In those days, the European countries were heavily forested. All the woodlands were sacred to Diana, especially oak groves. Diana was praised for her strength and athletic grace; her skill as a huntress was unsurpassed. Hunting skills were especially important to humans at this time, because they relied on meat as a main source of nourishment, especially in winter. Some statues show Diana with many breasts on her torso, symbolizing her ability to feed all creatures.

Diana is also a moon goddess. The changing moon reflects the changing cycles of nature, and as a goddess of wild, natural places, Diana is closely associated with her. The cycles of the moon influence all growing things, plants, animals, and humans alike. Diana reminds us of our connection with these cycles.

Diana's beauty made her the object of many men's love, but she preferred to be free and chose no man as her mate. Everyone respected her choice but one. Acteon so wanted Diana that he disguised himself in a deer skin and antlers, then hid behind an oak tree and spied on her while she bathed. Diana was not fooled and, in a fury, allowed her hunting dogs to tear him to pieces.

Some people believe that this story describes a hunting ritual performed at the beginning of winter to ensure there will be food, rather than a warning about the hot temper of an angry goddess. Acteon symbolizes the stag that men hoped they would find in the forests, since in those days they hunted stags for meat during the winter months. They prayed to Diana to help their hunting dogs to catch the stags, just as the dogs caught the unlucky Acteon.

Worship of Diana, goddess of hunting and of the moon, extended across Europe. She was still believed to rule the wild forests until the Middle Ages. Then, many people forgot that she was a goddess and called her queen of the witches instead. They had forgotten that she symbolized the Earth's ability to provide for all of its creatures, even in the coldest, harshest winter.

ESTSANATLEHI

In the southwestern United States, the most important deity that the Navajo people honor is Estsanatlehi (*est-san-AT-lu-hee*), a kind-hearted earth goddess. Estsanatlehi symbolizes the ever-changing earth on which plants grow, die, and are born again each year. Because the goddess appears as a young maiden for the spring and summer and an old woman for the fall and winter, her name means "woman who changes."

According to Navajo myth, Estsanatlehi was first discovered by human beings. A gray rain cloud led the first man and woman to the summit of a mountain, where they found Estsanatlehi. She was fed pollen by the sun and grew to be a woman in only eighteen days. Later, she became the wife of the sun. The Navajo believe that the sun visits her every evening at her sacred home in the west upon the great water.

Estsanatlehi's home is surrounded by four mountains. Each mountain is a replica of the north, south, east, and west boundaries of the Navajo nation. By dancing on each one in turn, Estsanatlehi creates rain clouds from the eastern mountain and beautiful fabrics and jewels from the southern. Her dance upon the western mountain provides plants of all kinds, while her northern dance creates corn and animals.

Estsanatlehi is also believed to be the creator of the Blessingway, a group of special Navajo rituals. The Blessingway is performed to create hope and good fortune for the participants. The songs and ceremonies which make up the Blessingway are used for weddings, childbirth rites, and many other happy occasions in the life of the Navajo. Each Blessingway takes place over several days and includes many songs, prayers, and ceremonial baths in yucca, or cactus, suds. Pulverized flower blossoms, cornmeal, and pollen are spread upon the earth to bless it and to bring good fortune to the Navajo nation. Estsanatlehi is said to be the author of all the songs and rituals used in the Blessingway.

FREYJA

In Norse mythology, gods and goddesses are divided into two groups, the Vanir and the Aesir. The peaceful Vanir grew food from the earth; they were worshiped during the agricultural Bronze Age. Then, in the Iron Age, when human beings developed the first weapons and hunting tools, the combative Aesir were worshiped. The Aesir brought war and discord into the peaceful world of the Vanir. To settle the war between them, the Vanir agreed to give the Aesir the goddess of beauty, Freyja (*FRAY-ah*), who was also the daughter of Njord, the god of fair winds.

In this way, Freyja became the link between the old world, before the invention of iron tools, and the new, as well as the mediator between peace and violence. She also became known as the goddess who presided over the living and the dead. Although she was honored mainly as a goddess of beauty and love, Freyja was also responsible for the souls of half of the warriors who died in battle. After their death, these men were taken to Freyja's grand hall in Asgard, the home of the Aesir gods and goddesses. The afterlife of warriors brought to Freyja was filled with joy and pleasure. They were brought delicious food and drink by her serving maidens and listened to the goddess's favorite poems about brave deeds.

Despite the cheerful company of her warriors, Freyja was often sad because her husband had mysteriously disappeared. Freyja had married Od, the god of ecstasy, but he vanished after the birth of their daughter, Noss, whose name means "delight." When Freyja missed her husband too much, she wept tears of gold. Sometimes she looked for Od, riding through the sky in her golden chariot drawn by two gray cats. At other times, she wore her falcon-skin cloak, which enabled her to fly through the air like a bird. Freyja was said never to be seen without her favorite necklace, given to her by the dwarves who mine precious metals and gems from the earth. So beautiful is this piece of jewelry that the Norse still refer to the Milky Way as "Freyja's necklace."

GWENHWYFAR

In Wales, white water waves are poetically called "the sheep of the Mermaid." That mermaid is the goddess Gwenhwyfar (*GWEN-eh-far*), the first lady of the Welsh islands and sea. She is said to have existed for as long as there was surf to pound against the rocky shore.

Some identify Gwenhwyfar as the daughter of the first Welsh bard, the Giant Ogyrvan. In Germany, she is called Cunneware, which means "female wisdom," and an early British history mentions a Roman lady named Guanhumara. But today most people recognize Gwenhwyfar as Queen Guinevere, the celebrated consort of King Arthur. Guinevere was the daughter of King Leodegrance of the North. When she wed Arthur, Guinevere brought with her and gave to her new husband a huge round oak table capable of seating one hundred and fifty knights. This round table was a wise gift, for while seated around it all knights were equal, since none could sit higher or lower than any other. It promoted peace among the warring knights and became an emblem of the golden age of Camelot, the castle from which Arthur governed his realm. King Arthur and his knights of the round table were famed for their brave and chivalrous deeds.

In Welsh mythology, Arthur was born of the goddess when he was cast ashore by the ninth wave of the sea. When it was time for him to die, he was brought back into the sea by Gwenhwyfar as she sang his death song. Welsh bards call such songs "giving back to the sea mother," or *marswygafen*.

Since Gwenhwyfar symbolized the throne of Wales, no king was able to rule without her by his side as once and future queen. It is little wonder that many would-be kings attempted to abduct her, since they foolishly thought that possessing the queen would make them king. Other legends say that after Arthur's death Gwenhwyfar retreated to her castle called Joyous Gard, where earthly paradise still exists. There she rules over her faithful subjects as Queen of the May each spring.

China

HSI WANG MU

The people of China honor Hsi Wang Mu (*SHEE WANG MUH*) as the goddess of eternal life. Hsi Wang Mu lives in a golden palace on Jade Mountain, in a heavenly land called Kun-lun. Red phoenixes and white cranes, both birds which symbolize long life, are said to live there with her. Since it is bordered on the west by a vast desert, only those who are invited may enter her domain.

But Hsi Wang Mu was not always the goddess of eternal life. Long ago, she was thought to be the bringer of plague and sickness. She was said to have wild black hair, the savage teeth of a tiger, and the long tail of a leopard. Her only companions were three strange, green birds who flew across the world of humans to find food for her and bring it back to her dark and lonely cave. No one knows how Hsi Wang Mu changed from a goddess of death to a goddess of life, but now she is remembered especially for her wonderful orchard of peaches.

Hsi Wang Mu is responsible for growing magical peaches which give eternal life to anyone who tastes them. She grows these peaches in an orchard within the enchanted gardens that surround her heavenly palace. It takes three thousand years for the peach trees in her enchanted orchard to come to fruit. During all this time, Hsi Wang Mu patiently tends them, like a mother caring for her children. This is why she is called the Royal Mother of the Western Paradise. The power of her peach trees is so remarkable that Chinese wizards used their branches for magic wands.

When the peaches are finally ripe, Hsi Wang Mu invites all the Chinese gods and goddesses to Jade Mountain for a picnic to celebrate her birthday. Together, they sit beside a magical fountain by a jewel-like lake and enjoy dish after dish of exotic foods such as bear paws, monkey lips and dragon livers. After the last bite has been taken, Hsi Wang Mu serves the peaches to her guests. By eating the fruit, they can be sure that they will live for another three thousand years in good health and happiness.

Egypt
Isis

For over 3000 years — from before 3000 B.C. to the second century A.D. — Isis (Eye-sis) was worshiped in Egypt as the Great Mother Goddess of the Universe. Isis took care of everything to do with wetness and moisture. She was present every day at sunrise, and at the time of the new and full moon. Her milk nourished all living beings. In this picture, Isis is wearing her traditional headdress with a sun-disk between two cow horns. Isis looked after the affairs of the day, while her sister, Nephthys, took care of the night. She also had two brothers, Osiris and Set. Osiris was responsible for the soil, and Set ruled the barren desert and the sea.

When they were old enough, the sun-god Ra married Isis to Osiris and Set to Nephthys. Isis and Osiris were blissful in their love. When Set noticed this, jealousy ate at his soul. He trapped his brother in a coffin and heaved him into the swirling waters of the Nile.

Turning herself into a kite, Isis flew everywhere searching for Osiris. Finally, she found the coffin embedded in a tree. Isis hid the coffin from Set. But Set found out. He cut Osiris's body into fourteen pieces and scattered them in all directions.

Isis traveled up and down the Nile in a papyrus boat, searching for the pieces of her lost lover. When she had found them all, she placed them next to each other. With the power of her love, she briefly brought Osiris back to life and conceived a child. That child became Horus, the falcon-headed god. Together, Isis and Horus were able to bring Set to justice for the murder of Osiris.

The myth of Isis and Osiris celebrates the changing cycles of the year — Osiris is the life-force of Nature which dies and is reborn, and Isis is the force of love that can create new life out of old. Today, we can see how this story helped the Egyptians to make sense of the world they lived in and to find an order and a pattern in the routine of their daily lives.

JUNO

The ancient Romans worshiped a supreme goddess they called Juno (*JOO-noh*). With her consort, the god Jupiter, Juno ruled over all aspects of Roman life. Besides being called Great Mother, she was also invoked as "Optima Maxima," meaning "best and greatest" of the goddesses.

Juno was believed to watch and protect all women from their first to last breath. For this reason, Roman women called their souls "juno" in honor of the goddess. Every year, on the first of March, the matrons, or married women, of Rome held a special festival called the *Matronalia* to praise Juno and thank her for her help. During this festival, they asked the goddess to bless their marriages and help them give birth to healthy babies.

To this day, many people consider the month of June, which is named after the goddess, to be the most favorable time to marry. As the patroness of marriage, Juno restored peace between quarreling couples. One of her temples was used as a sanctuary for women who needed shelter from cruel husbands.

Since she was originally a moon goddess, Juno was also worshiped as the giver of light on the night of the full moon. Round and full like a woman's womb carrying a child, the moon was believed to symbolize the ability of women to bear children, which Roman women thought to be the goddess's greatest concern. Accordingly, all newborn children were said to be blessed and guarded by Juno. The moon was also important to ancient societies because they relied on it as a calendar to tell them when to plant their crops for the most plentiful outcome.

The peacock is associated with Juno because the many eyes in its feathers are like the goddess's ever-open eyes as she watches over women. The richly colored plumes of the peacock were said to be like Juno's beautiful robes. Because of this, Roman men and women carried *flabella*, ornate fans made out of peacock feathers, during the sacred rites of Juno.

KUAN YIN

Honored as the holy mother of compassion and mercy, Kuan Yin (*KWAN yin*) is one of the most beloved goddesses of China. She is said to personify karuna, the principle of boundless compassion and loving kindness. Considered the guardian angel of humans and the patroness of mothers and seamen, she is often depicted sitting on a lotus, the flower of enlightenment, with a child next to her. Many people believe that even to say the goddess's name will bring protection and relief to those in need of her help.

One story says that before she became a goddess, Kuan Yin was the youngest of three daughters of a cruel father. When she saw her father force her sisters to marry unkind but wealthy husbands, Kuan Yin asked to enter a temple instead. Her father agreed, but secretly ordered the temple residents to give Kuan Yin the hardest chores, to discourage her. Kuan Yin had so much to do that after toiling all day, she had to work all night while the others slept.

But the animals who lived near the temple saw Kuan Yin's hardships and decided to help her. The tigers gathered wood for the fire. The snakes brought water to the temple. The birds collected vegetables from the garden, while the spirit of fire cooked food for everyone. News of these miracles spread from the lonely temple and reached her cruel father. In a fury, he set fire to the temple. But Kuan Yin put out the fire with her hands alone, without suffering one burn. Finally, her father gave orders for her to be killed for disobedience.

After her death, Kuan Yin was brought to heaven, where her purity of heart and mercy toward others transformed her into a goddess. But just as she was about to cross heaven's threshold, she heard a cry. It was someone suffering down on earth. Moved by pity, Kuan Yin asked to be sent back to earth to help anyone in need. She vowed never to leave until the last human being was free from pain. Many people believe that Kuan Yin is still among us, looking after the many humans in need of her care.

LAKSHMI

Lakshmi (*LAKSH-meè*) is especially treasured in India as the goddess of good fortune, prosperity, and beauty. She is believed to represent all that is feminine, while her consort, Vishnu, who is called the conqueror of darkness, represents all that is masculine. Many paintings from India show Lakshmi and Vishnu riding on the back of Garuda the eagle, the giant king of birds, as they fly across the land.

According to Indian mythology, Lakshmi was created from the Ocean of Milk. Vishnu churned the Ocean of Milk for Indra, king of the gods, because he wanted to make a magic potion that would bestow eternal life. As he churned the ocean, many wonderful things came out of it, including a wish-giving cow and tree, an elephant, a handsome white horse, and a matchless jewel. Most precious of all was the beautiful goddess Lakshmi.

Lakshmi rose out of the Ocean of Milk standing on a lotus flower, with a lotus blossom in her hand and a crown of lotuses on her pale brow. The goddess immediately announced that her place was next to Vishnu's heart. So Lakshmi and Vishnu were married and soon had a son, whom they named Kama. Kama came to be considered the god of romantic love. In many paintings, he looks similar to the cupids on Valentine cards which we give to show our love to another person.

As the goddess of good fortune, Lakshmi is said to be attracted to sparkling jewels, which are like the riches she bestows on her worshipers. Some people believe that she lives in the sky with the most beautiful jewels of all, the stars. Once a year, on the night of the new moon in November, Indian women clean their homes and hang tiny lanterns outside that look like stars themselves. They hope that these lanterns will attract the goddess to their homes and that she will bless them with good fortune and prosperity for the coming year.

MAIA

When we look into the night sky, we can recognize the seven stars which make up the constellation called the Pleiades. The ancient Greeks thought that these stars were once the seven daughters of Atlas, and that the goddess Maia (*MAY-ah*) was the youngest of them. When he took part in a revolt led by the giants against the gods of Olympus, Atlas was made to bear the world on his shoulders as punishment. Maia and her sisters mourned their father's humiliation so much that the gods turned them into doves to spare them any more pain. Then they flew to the highest heaven and became brightly shining stars — the seven stars we call the Pleiades.

Maia is mainly remembered today as the goddess of spring and rebirth, like the month of May that bears her name. "Maia" means "the maker," and every spring she makes the lush green grass and the fragrant flowers grow again. She is also praised as "the grandmother of magic" because her son, the god Hermes, was the first to discover that mysterious art.

Soon after Maia gave birth to Hermes, she knew her son was a genius. While still a crawling baby, he created the first lyre by stretching strings across a tortoise shell, and the first panpipe from marsh reeds. Besides being the first magician, Hermes is credited with the invention of medicine, astrology, and letters. Part of his duties as messenger to the gods and goddesses was the responsibility of bringing the souls of the dead to the underworld. It is interesting to see how through this function Maia's son became the god of death, which contrasts to Maia's role as bringer of life each spring.

People still celebrate Maia every year on the first of May, which is called May Day in honor of the goddess. Men and women rejoice over the rebirth of spring by dancing circles around the maypole and by wearing vibrant green — the color of the earth itself.

Java

NYAI LORO KIDUL

The royal family of the island of Java believe that their divine right to rule was bestowed on them by Nyai Loro Kidul (*Nahi LOW-row KEH-dul*), the mermaid goddess of the South Seas. A popular story says that this goddess married the king of Java in the sixteenth century. Before returning to the sea, she taught the king how to gain the power of the spirits, so that he could rule Java wisely. Since then, all rulers of Java have considered Nyai Loro Kidul their divine ancestress.

Nyai Loro Kidul is believed to have been the mortal daughter of a king of Java in ancient times. Upon her mother's death, her father remarried unwisely. The princess's new stepmother was wildly jealous of her, and with the aid of an evil wizard poisoned her stepdaughter's bathwater so that her skin erupted in painful sores. The poor princess was banished to the forests. She wandered there for a long time until she came to the south shore of the island. While she rested on the ocean's edge, an ethereal voice called to her from beneath the moonlit waves. "Come and rest here," the voice said. "Here you shall be a mighty queen, regain your beauty, and rule the green ocean forever." Immediately, the princess threw herself into the sea, where she was transformed into the radiant goddess Nyai Loro Kidul.

The Javanese still honor Nyai Loro Kidul today. As a seductive mermaid queen, her powers reflect the mysterious hidden forces of the ocean. Local people know better than to swim in the waters on the south shore of Java, where the goddess is said to reside. It is believed that she looks out for mortals to serve her in her undersea realm and is especially enticed by young men wearing green bathing trunks. To appease the goddess, people leave offerings of coconuts, clothes, and fingernail clippings at the ocean's edge, all of which are eagerly accepted by the powerful sea.

O y a

The Yoruba people of Nigeria believe that the Niger River is ruled by a powerful goddess named Oya (*oy-YAH*). When Oya is happy, the river flows smoothly, bringing clear water to nurture the many families who depend on it. But when she is angry, then the river may overflow or run dry. Oya also sends storm winds to warn the guilty of the approach of her husband, Shango, the thunder god, from his copper palace in the sky. The winds Oya creates are strong enough to tear the roofs off houses and uproot huge trees.

One story tells that Oya was originally an antelope and was able to take off her skin as you or I would take off a coat. Then, looking like any woman, she would go to the marketplace to spend time among humans. It was there that the thunder god Shango first saw Oya and lost his heart to her. He hid her antelope skin and married her. It did not take long for wise Oya to find out where her husband had put her precious antelope skin. But Shango begged her forgiveness and in apology offered *akara*, special bean cakes, to her. Akara were Oya's favorite food, so she was delighted. She agreed to stay with Shango and help him fight his battles against those who vexed him.

Since words are made of the wind that we make when we breathe, and since Oya is praised for her persuasive, charming speech, Yoruba women often ask the goddess for help choosing the right words to ease conflicts and gain power. It is because of this that Oya is considered the patroness of female leadership.

To please Oya, many Yoruba wear strings of long maroon beads around their necks. They keep altars in the corner of their homes displaying objects sacred to her: buffalo or "bush cow" horns and a copper crown symbolizing the copper palace where she lives with Shango, and the bean cakes she loves. Sometimes, they place statues of her wearing a headdress decorated with copper nails that looks like Shango's thunder axe. Oya is still widely worshiped among the Yoruba.

PELE

In the Hawaiian islands, where there are many volcanoes, people believe in a tempestuous goddess of fire called Pele (*PEH-leh*). Pele rules over all kinds of fire, but especially over the lava that flows from erupting volcanoes. The finest strands of molten lava are called "Pele's hair."

Everyday life would be very harsh without fire to cook food or to heat homes in winter. But humans also live in fear of fires devastating their homes and forests. Like fire itself, Pele has the power to destroy as well as to create. If she is pleased by the islanders' prayers, she will generously check the flow of hot lava toward a village. But if she is angered, she will turn people and animals to stone. Hawaiians also believe that earthquakes are caused by an angry stomp of Pele's foot.

Pele was created by the heat of the earth, like lava from a volcano. Surprisingly, her first home was in the sea, with her sister, a sea goddess. But she grew angry with Pele and drove her away. Pele wandered across the sea for a time, then she came to Hawaii. There, she is thought to have settled in Mount Kilauea, one of the most active volcanoes in the world.

Hawaiians believe that to amuse herself, Pele sometimes visits them. With a back as straight as a cliff and breasts as round as the moon, she is described by those who have seen her as the most beautiful woman on earth. Her royal bearing and great charm make her irresistible. One story from long ago tells how Prince Lohiau, the chief of the island of Kaua'i, fell deeply in love with Pele during one of her visits. Unaware that the object of his love was the fire goddess, the prince insisted that they marry immediately. Since Pele loved him also, she agreed. Three days after the wedding, Pele left her new husband to arrange her affairs, promising to return as quickly as she could. But she took too long. Prince Lohiau, thinking she had abandoned him, died of a broken heart. His encounter with the goddess had been as destructive as the volcano's fire.

QUEEN OF HEAVEN

Inanna, (*ee-NAN-nah*) the great goddess of the Bronze Age, was honored with the title "Queen of Heaven." She was said to be clothed with the stars and to wear the rainbow as her necklace while the zodiac wrapped itself round her waist as a belt, and the crescent moon crowned her head. Inanna is often depicted standing regally upon two winged lions, showing her divinity. In Sumeria, where she was worshiped five thousand years ago, her temple was called "Eanna," which means "house of heaven."

Inanna was credited with power over many aspects of Sumerian life. Besides ruling over the stars and planets in the heavens, she was also goddess of the rain clouds which gave the water needed for grain to grow. Because they believed that all moisture was caused by the moon, the Sumerians also thought that Inanna was responsible for the cool, lunar rays of light that carried precious dew to the earth during the night. Since Sumeria, which is today Iraq, is a land scorched by sun, it is understandable how valuable a goddess who created water would be.

Inanna's name translates as "Queen Moon," and the story of her descent to the land of the dead explains her connection with the moon. Inanna's older sister, Ereshkigal, was the goddess of the dead and ruled over Kur-nu-gi-a, the land without return below the sweet waters of the earth. One day, Inanna, Queen of Heaven, descended to the land of the dead to visit her sister. But Ereshkigal killed her visitor and hung her corpse upon a stake. While Inanna was gone, the moon disappeared from the night sky and all things ceased to grow upon the earth. After three days, the water god obtained access to Inanna's corpse. He sprinkled it with the water of life, resurrecting Inanna, and she returned to the upper world, bringing the moon and all of life back with her. From this story, we can see how Inanna's trip to and from the land of the dead describes the waning and waxing of the moon.

RHIANNON

In Berkshire, England, there is a huge impression of a horse carved in the chalk on the side of a hill. This enormous white carving, dating from the first century B.C., shows the immense importance of the horse to people of that time. Horses were used for traveling, plowing fields, and transporting heavy loads. So it is not surprising that the British horse goddess Rhiannon (*REE-an-non*) was said to appear to her followers riding an unearthly white horse, like the horse carved in the side of the hill.

Dressed in royal robes of gold, Rhiannon is always accompanied by three birds from the Happy Otherworld, where gods and goddesses live. The magical song of these birds could lull the living to death, restore the dead to life, and heal all sadness and pain.

Rhiannon's name is derived from "rigantona," which means "great queen goddess." In an earlier period, she was known as Epona. Many statues have been found of her as Epona. Most of them show her with a mare on one side and a bundle of grain on the other, showing her connection to the harvest. Other statues depict a mare, foal, and goddess.

Rhiannon is an important character in *The Mabinogion*, a collection of Welsh myths from the thirteenth century. One of these myths tells the story of how Pwyll, the prince of Dyfed, fell in love with the goddess after spying her on her white horse. Pwyll guessed from her ethereal quality that she was of enchanted origin, but he was undaunted. Determined to catch up on her, he rode his horse as fast as he could. But no matter how fast he rode — or how slowly Rhiannon appeared to ride — he was unable to reach her. This went on for many days. Finally, the humbled prince called to the goddess to wait for him, which she did. When he asked "Why didn't you stop earlier?" she simply replied, "Why didn't you ask me?"

After this, the couple lived happily together for many years.

India
SARASVATI

Because she is the goddess of all knowledge, Sarasvati (*sa-RAS-vah-tee*) is held in special esteem by students, writers, and musicians. She is credited in India with the creation of the fruits of civilization: the first alphabet, the arts, mathematics, music, and magic. Extraordinarily beautiful and graceful, Sarasvati is easily recognizable by her dazzling white skin and brilliant clothing. Her color and brightness is said to represent the powerful, pure light of education which destroys the darkness of ignorance.

One myth tells how Sarasvati and her consort, Brahma, were born from a golden egg which came from the sea. They then created all of the knowledge and all of the creatures in the world. Many also consider Sarasvati the mother of all life since it was her divine energy, united with the awareness of Brahma, which brought everything into being.

Sarasvati is also a river goddess and her name translates as "the flowing one." In India, the pure, flowing waters of rivers represent the purifying and nurturing waters of life, and are still regarded as sacred. Sarasvati shares her name with a river that flows down from the Himalayan mountains to join the Ganges River.

Many pictures of Sarasvati show her seated upon a lotus-blossom throne, accompanied by a white swan. The swan is believed to be able to separate milk from water in the same bowl — an act which shows the ability to discriminate between actions and offerings that are good and wise and those that are insincere. Sarasvati is depicted with four arms, showing that her power extends in all directions. In one of her hands she holds a book and in the other a strand of beads. The book represents learning, while the beads indicate spiritual knowledge. With her other hands she holds and plays the vina, an Indian lute, representing the art of music.

Tibet
TARA

The most important deity for Tibetan Buddhists is the compassionate mother goddess Tara (*tah-rah*). Tibetans believe that Tara has the power to heal all sorrows and grant all wishes. The name "Tara" translates as "she who causes one to cross," which means that the goddess will help her devotees to cross safely to the other side of a troublesome situation.

Tibetan Buddhists approach life as a process which enables them to gain inner wisdom and knowledge. They believe this inner wisdom leads to true happiness and peace, which is better than any riches the world can offer. Such an enlightened person is called a buddha, or "blessed one." The goddess Tara was once a woman who yearned to gain this enlightenment and became the first female buddha. One story says that she worked and prayed for the welfare of humans everywhere for over ten million years before she reached her goal. Then she was transformed into a goddess whose only wish was to ease the world's pain.

Tara is honored as the protectress against the many fears that block men and women from living in happiness and harmony. Some of her roles reveal the kind of fears that concerned the people of old Tibet. For example, Tara is said to protect her followers from the fear of elephants and poisonous snakes, and an old legend tells how she saved a wood-gatherer from a hungry lioness. When the wood-gatherer called for help, Tara appeared to him dressed in forest leaves and pulled him from the jaws of the lioness. Then she returned the man safely to the marketplace!

But other fears from which Tara offers protection are those that everyone can identify with. Who has never felt the fear of poverty, unfair imprisonment, or theft? Tara will not only protect her followers, but she will also save all those who cry her name at the moment of their suffering. Tara is Tibet's most popular deity and is still widely worshiped.

Japan
UKEMOCHI

The Japanese once believed that all the food of the earth was created by Ukemochi (*U-kee-MOH-chee*), a gentle and kind goddess. No one was ever short of food because of Ukemochi's generosity. The Japanese also believed that, instead of being separated by night and day, the sun and moon lived peacefully together in a palace in the heavens. This changed, however, because of a task which was set to the moon god by the sun goddess Amaterasu.

One day, Amaterasu commanded her brother, the moon god Tsuki-yomi, to go down to earth to visit Ukemochi and make certain that the food goddess was performing her duties correctly. Ukemochi was so excited and honored by the prospect of Tsuki-yomi's visit that she prepared a grand feast for him. First, she turned her head to the land, and rice rushed forth from her mouth. Then she turned to the sea, and all kinds of fish spilled onto the banquet table, deliciously prepared for the moon god. Finally, Ukemochi turned toward the high mountains. Within moments, all sorts of meats emerged from her mouth and arranged themselves in as rich a feast as ever was.

But Tsuki-yomi was not impressed by Ukemochi's generous offering of food from her body. Tsuki-yomi was disgusted. He drew his sword and stabbed her.

Even in death, Ukemochi continued to create food. As she lay dying, her head turned into cows and horses, who ran off to populate the earth. Grain sprouted from her forehead, and its seed blew into the fields and grew. Then rice plants sprouted from the goddess's belly. Her inky eyebrows became silkworms, whose threads were woven into rainbow-colored silks to clothe the gods and goddesses.

And so Ukemochi's body lived on in many forms, providing nourishment for everyone. When Amaterasu, the sun goddess, learned that her brother had killed the gentle food goddess, her fury was without limits. From that time on, the moon god has avoided being in the palace when Amaterasu is awake. And that is why the sun is out during the day, and the moon only at night.

VENUS

Venus (*VEE-nus*) was the name the ancient Romans gave to the goddess of love. Created from the union of sea and sky, Venus was born of sea foam and water and was described as "the star of the sea" by her worshipers. As the goddess of love, she was "the queen of pleasure;" she was also honored as the mother of the Roman people.

Venus was married to Vulcan, the lame god of the forge. She was also closely associated with Mars, the god of war, but it was with a mortal man, Anchises, that she gave birth to Aeneas. Aeneas was a Trojan prince who escaped after the fall of Troy and sailed to Italy, where he became the founder of Rome. During his many adventures, which were recorded in *The Aeneid* by the poet Virgil, Aeneas was protected by enchanted armor that his mother persuaded Vulcan to make for him.

Venus is the goddess who inspires people to love each other and to have children, ensuring that the human race continues to grow. She is also a nature goddess, associated with the arrival of spring. When Venus approaches, winds die away, clouds scatter, flowers spring from the ground, the sea smiles, and brightness fills the sky. At her entrance, all living creatures in sky and sea are struck to the heart by her power and happily follow wherever she leads. Venus is the bringer of joy to gods and humans as well as to the plant world. For hundreds of years, artists and poets have turned to her for inspiration. The Italian artist Botticelli painted a magnificent picture called *The Birth of Venus*, and the playwright and poet William Shakespeare also sang her praises.

Shrines have been built to Venus in many parts of the Mediterranean. The city of Venice, in north Italy, is named after her, and each year the people of Venice celebrate the marriage of their city to the goddess by throwing a golden wedding ring into the sea. This ceremony ensures that Venus will protect the city and help its people to prosper.

Australia
WAWALAK

Before Europeans colonized Australia, over four hundred nomadic tribes inhabited the continent. Today, their numbers are much reduced, but these aboriginal peoples still believe that the world was created in a mythic past called "the dreamtime." During the dreamtime, the gods and goddesses who were sleeping beneath the ground awoke and wandered over the earth. As they traveled, they created the landscape and all living creatures, and taught them the art of survival. Once the world was completed, these divine ancestors went back to sleep in their underground abode.

Of all the aboriginal gods and goddesses, one of the most renowned is Yurlungur, the Great Rainbow Serpent. Yurlungur is called the great mother and father, and is responsible for the bringing of rain. The myth of the Wawalak (*WAH-wah-lak*), two sister goddesses of north Australia, illustrates the power of these fertility goddesses against the Great Rainbow Serpent.

During the dreamtime, the Wawalak traveled from the south to the north with their two newborn babies and set up camp next to the water hole of the Great Rainbow Serpent. Unaware that the water hole was sacred, the goddesses accidentally polluted the waters with a single drop of blood. The pool flooded and rains poured down in an angry response. To appease the heavens and protect their babies, the Wawalak sang and sang, but they could not sing forever. Finally, Yurlungur came out of the water hole and swallowed the Wawalak in a huge gulp, babies and all. Later, he felt ashamed when he thought about what he had done to the goddesses. So he opened his great mouth. Out came the Wawalak, and they lived once more.

Since then, the place where the Wawalak and their babies were reborn from the Great Rainbow Serpent has been a sacred spot for religious ceremonies. As both goddesses and mothers, the Wawalak symbolize the unending force of life in all women, a force that can never be stilled.

Xochiquetzal

The Aztecs, a people who ruled over a vast empire in Mexico during the Middle Ages, believed in a flower goddess who they called Xochiquetzal (*sho-chee-KET-sal*). The goddess's sacred flower was the yellow marigold; her name meant "feather flower," probably referring to the marigold's many fine, feathery petals. One of the merriest of the Aztec deities, Xochiquetzal was also the goddess of dance, music, crafts, and love. Appropriately, her twin brother, Xochipilli, was honored as the god of pleasure.

Xochiquetzal was said to live on top of a mountain above the nine heavens. This flowery garden paradise was populated by merry dwarves, dancing maidens, and musicians. The Aztec believed that anyone who was faithful to the goddess would spend eternity in her paradise when their earthly life had ended.

Xochiquetzal was married to the rain god Tlaloc. The moisture that Tlaloc created in the skies helped her flowers to grow. Though many men fell in love with Xochiquetzal because of her beauty and her happy nature, she remained loyal to her husband for many years. But finally, the persistent and mischievous god Texcatlipoca won her away from Tlaloc. According to Aztec mythology, Texcatlipoca loved Xochiquetzal so much that he sang of the goddess, "She seems to me a very queen, she is so lovely and so gay."

The Aztec also told a myth about a flood which destroyed all creatures except for Xochiquetzal and one mortal man. To repopulate the earth, they had many children, but all of them were born voiceless. But Xochiquetzal willed a dove to descend from the tree of heaven. The dove gave each child a voice and a language, then the children were scattered across the globe. The Aztecs believed that all of the different races and languages in the world sprang from these children. With this story, they honored Xochiquetzal as the mother of the world.

Cuba

YEMANA

Yemana (*yay-MAN-ah*), the Santeria goddess of the ocean, is believed to be the daughter of the earth goddess Oddudua and the sister and wife of the god Aganju. As the divine mother of the fourteen gods and goddesses who make up the sacred pantheon, she occupies an exalted position in the Santeria religion.

Santeria developed from the Yoruba religion practiced by enslaved Africans who were brought to Cuba to work on the sugar-cane plantations during the nineteenth century. Because these unfortunate people were not allowed to worship as they wished, they mingled the symbolism and traditions of their native gods and goddesses with that of the saints from the widely followed and accepted Roman Catholic teachings. The Santeria religion spread from Cuba, where it originated, through the Caribbean and out to North and South America. It is still widely practiced today.

Since Yemana is the beautiful and immensely powerful goddess of the waters, many people who follow her call her "Holy Queen Sea." She is said to own all the riches of the ocean: seashells, pearls, oysters, coral reefs, and every sea creature. As the goddess of water, she is also called on to bring rain.

Yemana is also revered as the great mother of all as the sea is like the waters of the womb from which all humans are born. As the goddess of motherhood, she is associated with Christianity's Virgin Mary. Women who wish for children will often ask for her help.

At some time in their lives, each practitioner of Santeria takes one of the gods or goddesses to be their spiritual mother or father and tries to develop a special relationship with him or her. Those who are the children of Yemana try to please the goddess in many ways. Since seven is the number sacred to Yemana, they wear seven silver bracelets on their arms. They also burn candles as blue as the seas Yemana rules, and wear beautiful blue and crystal beads strung into necklaces in honor of the goddess.

ZORYA

In myths all over the world there have always been trinities of goddesses who are believed to influence and bear responsibility for the well-being of the earth. Usually these three goddesses also symbolize the three ages of women, these being maiden, mother, and old woman.

The ancient Greeks believed in three goddesses they called the Fates. These mysterious beings were said to write the world's future, which mere humans had to wait to see unfold. In Scandinavian mythology, the three Norns wove the thread of life which, if it broke, would bring the end of the world. The Zorya (*ZOR-yah*), with whom we end this book of goddesses, are such a trio.

In Russian mythology, the three Zorya represent, and are named after, different times of day. The first goddess is called Dawn, the second Twilight, and the third Midnight. The Zorya are attendants of the sun-god, who rides through the sky on his horse every day, bringing light and warmth to the earth. The sun-god is said to return each evening to a magical isle ruled by the Zorya. When he is ready to leave the isle at daybreak, Dawn opens the gates of heaven to let him out. Since the sun-god sets out in the morning and gradually grows older during the day, by nightfall he is an old man when he returns to the Zorya's magical isle, where Twilight closes the gates behind him. Then he is born again as a new baby during the night, ready to repeat the cycle.

As well as attending to the sun-god, without whose light all living things would perish, the Zorya are believed to be the guardians of the universe. As such, the goddesses are responsible for guarding a terrible doomsday hound, which is chained to the constellation of the Little Bear. According to Russian mythology, the end of the world would be at hand if ever the chain were to break.

SOURCE BOOKS

The art and words offered in *The Book of Goddesses* are the product of many hours of work and research. I wove the goddesses' stories from various sources, and in doing so searched for an illustrative approach that would honor each tradition. Eventually I decided that the best way to do this would be to paint the goddesses as women, with the clothing, jewelry and demeanor appropriate to their native cultures.

I hope that the following bibliography will inspire you to read on to discover other goddesses from around the world. The titles listed here were of particular help to me while I worked on this book.

Baring, Anne, and Jules Cashford. *The Myth of the Goddess.* Viking Books, 1992.

Bascom, William. *The Yoruba of Southwestern Nigeria.* Holt, Rinehart, and Winston, 1969.

Beier, Ulli. *Yoruba Myths.* Cambridge University Press, 1980.

Bierhorst, John. *The Mythology of North America.* Quill/William Morrow, 1985.

Bolen, Jean Shinoda. *Goddesses in Everywoman.* HarperCollins, 1985.

Bulfinch, Thomas. *Bulfinch's Mythology.* Signet/New American Library, 1962.

Carlyon, Richard. *A Guide to the Gods.* Quill/William Morrow, 1981.

Carmody, Denise Lardner. *Mythological Woman: Contemporary Reflections on Ancient Religious Stories.* Crossroad, 1992.

Christie, Anthony. *Chinese Mythology.* Hamlyn Publishing Group, 1968.

Crossley-Holland, Kevin. *The Norse Myths.* Pantheon Fairy Tale and Folklore Library, 1980.

D'Aulaire, Ingri, and Edgar Parin. *D'Aulaire's Norse Gods and Giants.* Doubleday, 1967.

Erhman, Adolf. *Life in Ancient Egypt.* Dover Publications, 1971.

Gadon, Elinor W. *The Once and Future Goddess.* Harper and Row, 1989.

Gonzalez-Wippler, Migene. *The Santeria Experience.* Original Publications, 1982.

Grant, Michael. *Myths of the Greeks and Romans.* Harry N. Abrams, 1962.

Grimal, Pierre, editor. *Larousse World Mythology.* Hamlyn Publishing Group, 1968.

Harding, M. Esther. *Woman's Mysteries: Ancient and Modern.* Harper Perennial Library, 1976.

Hooke, S. H. *Middle Eastern Mythology: From the Assyrians to the Hebrews.* Penguin Books, 1963.

Hubbs, Joanna. *Mother Russia: The Feminine Myth in Russian Culture.* Indiana University Press, 1988.

Isaacs, Jennifer. *Arts of the Dreaming: Australia's Living Heritage.* Weldon Publishing, 1990.

Jaffrey, Madhur. *Seasons of Splendor: Tales, Myths and Legends of India.* Puffin Books, 1987.

Ke, Yuan. *Dragons and Dynasties: An Introduction to Chinese Mythology.* Penguin Books, 1993.

Kluckhorn, Clyde, and Dorothea Leighton. *The Navaho.* Doubleday Anchor, 1962.

Kraemer, Ross Shepard. *Her Share of the Blessings: Woman's Religions Among Pagans, Jews, and Christians in the Greco-Roman World.* Oxford University Press, 1992.

Kramer, Samuel Noah. *Mythologies of the Ancient World.* Anchor Books, 1961.

Locke, Raymond Friday. *The Book of the Navajo.* Mankind Publishing Company, 1992.

MacCana, Proisias. *Celtic Mythology.* Peter Bedrick Books, 1983.

McNeely, Jeffrey A., and Paul Spencer Wachtel. *Soul of the Tiger.* Doubleday, 1988.

Nicholson, Irene. *Mexican and Central American Mythology.* Hamlyn Publishing Group, 1975.

Nicholson, Shirley. *The Goddess Re-awakening.* Quest Books, 1989.

Osborne, Harold. *South American Mythology.* Hamlyn Publishing Group, 1969.

Parrinder, Geofrey. *African Mythology.* Hamlyn Publishing Group, 1969.

Piggott, Juliet. *Japanese Mythology.* Peter Bedrich Books, 1991.

Perowne, Steward. *Roman Mythology.* Peter Bedrich Books, 1988.

Pomeroy, Sarah B. *Goddesses, Whores, Wives, and Slaves: Woman in Classical Antiquity.* Schoken Books, 1975.

Rutherford, Ward. *Celtic Lore: The History of the Druids and their Timeless Traditions.* HarperCollins, 1993.

Shearer, Alistair. *Forms of the Formless: The Hindu Vision.* Thames and Hudson, 1993.

Spretnak, Charlene. *Lost Goddesses of Early Greece.* Beacon Press, 1992.

Stone, Merlin. *When God was a Woman.* Harvest/Harcourt Brace Jovanovich Books, 1976.

Sykes, Egerton. *Who's Who: Non-Classical Mythology.* Oxford University Press, 1993.

Walker, Barbara G. *The Woman's Encyclopedia of Myths and Secrets.* Harper San Francisco, 1983.

Wolkstein, Diane. *The First Love Stories.* HarperCollins, 1991.

Young, Serinity, editor. *An Anthology of Sacred Texts By and About Women.* Crossroad Publishing Company, 1993.

Kris Waldherr has illustrated and written several well-received picture books. Her most recent, *Persephone and the Pomegranate*, was praised by Jean Shinoda Bolen, M.D., author of *Goddesses in Everywoman*, as "a beautifully done retelling of the major mother-daughter myth" and by *The New York Times Book Review* for its "quality of myth and magic." Kris Waldherr's strong interest in mythology and folklore, especially women's myths, led to the extensive research which became *The Book of Goddesses*.

Kris Waldherr was born in West Haverstraw, New York, and received her bachelor of fine arts degree from the School of Visual Arts in New York City. She lived in Devon, England, while working on the paintings for her first book, *Rapunzel*, retold by Amy Ehrlich. *Rapunzel* was called "a visually resonant work, rich in enchantment and romance," by *Publishers Weekly*.

Kris Waldherr now lives in New York City. Her artwork has been shown throughout the United States and Great Britain.

Linda Schierse Leonard, Ph.D., is a Jungian analyst trained in Zurich who gives workshops, lectures, and consultations across the United States. She is the author of several highly praised books including *The Wounded Woman, On the Way to the Wedding, Witness to the Fire: Creativity and the Veil of Addiction, Meeting the Madwoman: Empowering the Feminine Spirit,* and *Creation's Heartbeat: Following the Reindeer Spirit.*